Making the Match

A practical guide to U.S Residency for International Medical Graduates

ADEMOLA ADEREMI ADESEYE MD, MPH

DEDICATION

To my mum Ibironke Adeseye: thank you for being
a rock of support through the years

To my lovely Princess, Christele. I love you

CONTENTS

ACKNOWLEDGMENTS

Family is everything. To my Dad Reverend Canon Damola Adeseye and my two wonderful siblings Adekunbi and Damola Jr: thank you so much for all you have done and continue to do in support of my goals. I love you

I remain eternally grateful to all those who have contributed in no little way to my progress in life: my mentor and friend Tabitha Garwe PhD, Roxie Albrecht MD, Jason Lees MD, William Havron III MD, Alexander Raines MD, Jeremy Johnson MD. Thank you!

INTRODUCTION

The experience of the average International Medical Graduate (IMG) or Foreign Medical Graduate (FMG) seeking to pursue medical practice in the United States is one that can only be understood by the IMG, or by a handful of people who somehow have gained insight into the unique IMG experience. Interestingly, IMGs also differ widely in their understanding of the entire process that leads up to securing a residency position in the US.

In this book, I aim to share with you a summary of my experiences in my transition from Nigeria to Medical Practice in the United States. Every aspiring candidate has circumstances and experiences that are unique to that candidate. The goal of this book is not to address every possible scenario, rather it is an attempt at summarizing my unique personal experiences while pointing out some common themes that define success or otherwise. In achieving the goal of US residency, there are several individuals who have taken paths completely different from mine, resulting in even more impressive outcomes than I can lay claim too. As such, this book does not say it all! On the contrary, it is aimed at preparing the mind of the reader for the task ahead.

My primary audience is International Medical Graduates (IMG) - a nomenclature used in the United States to describe Medical Doctors who obtained their medical degree outside the continental United States. IMGs are also sometimes referred to as FMGs (Foreign Medical Graduates). Though most IMGs are non-US citizens/permanent residents, the 'foreignness' of IMGs refers strictly to having obtained their medical degree outside the US. As such, US citizens/permanent residents who pursue medical education in the Caribbean Islands, an increasingly common trend, are also IMGs.

IMGs constitute a group of talented individuals with an ambition to practice medicine in the US. An ambition that is often either slowed in its fulfillment by the rocky path to residency or stifled by the sheer extent of the challenges IMGs must surmount. The monstrosity of the challenge, in my opinion, is grossly under appreciated by most.

This book is written primarily for IMGs (both students currently enrolled in a medical school outside the US as well as those who have already

obtained their degrees) as well as students who plan

to study medicine outside of the US with a goal of

pursuing residency training in the states. However,

it will also come in handy for Program Directors of

residency programs, Departmental Chairs of clinical

services, parents of IMGs and anyone else who

seeks to gain an understanding into the challenges

that the average IMG faces in pursuit of the goal of

residency training in the US.

By God's grace, I have had the opportunity to

counsel innumerable IMGs from multiple countries

including Nigeria, Cameroun, Rwanda, Ukraine,

Burkina Faso, Poland and the Caribbean Islands.

One month hardly goes by without me having to set

aside time to counsel an IMG regarding the path to

residency. My perennial conversations with these

talented Doctors is what inspired this book. My goal

is to share some key lessons with an even broader

audience via this book and help as many as I

possibly can.

1 **AMBITION**

AMBITION is enthusiasm with a purpose.

-Frank Tyger

As I reflect on why I chose to be a doctor and why I chose to pursue my surgical training in the United States, it all comes down to one word: AMBITION. I had the ambition to be a medical doctor and save lives. I had the ambition of training at Nigeria's first and best University - The University of Ibadan. I wanted to be the doctor that 'heals by hand' and restores function by surgically correcting anatomy. I wanted to be the doctor with unparalleled education, training and expertise who could give his patients the best care. I had the ambition of training with the best technology and exchanging ideas with leaders in the field of medicine and surgery. I wanted to get surgical training in the United States. I wanted to be at the top! Ambition is a good thing. Without ambition, mediocrity is certain and even if you stumble upon some level of success, it will only be short lived.

Ambition fuels the fire on the altar of success. An altar with an insatiable appetite for the most precious sacrificial offerings: Time being one of the most important sacrifices. I have spent the last two decades of my life in pursuit of my goals. I have friends who have chosen to pursue non-medical careers. These friends of mine have been working and successfully building their careers and families for over a decade while I still 'went to school'.

Ambition has helped me remain happy for their successes and life achievements, while maintaining our friendship. Ambition helped me keep my head down, pursue my dreams and take my time in starting a family.

As a resident, I have taught several medical students as they go through their surgery clinical rotations. While I am still putting in several years of being a surgery trainee, some of these medical students went on to pursue careers in Internal Medicine and Pediatrics, and are currently attendings in their respective fields. Ambition keeps me going.

I have family members who, after years of silently wondering what I was up to, have ceased wondering, instead they have started asking 'when will you be done with all this studying?' Ambition keeps the smile on my face as I patiently explain the complexities of surgical training. No answer of mine suffices for some family members and they still wonder 'why does he do all this?'.

Years after the idea was conceived, ambition helped me write the first words of this book. Ambition is a good thing!

AMBITION never comes to an end.
-Kenneth Kaunda

2 WHY RESIDENCY IN THE US?

Why do I want to pursue residency in the United States?

This question is particularly important for IMGs currently practicing as medical doctors in their home country or any other country and are contemplating further training in the US. You need to be able to verbalize succinctly, why you are ready to make a big career move. A move that pretty much involves transitioning from the known to the unknown. Being able to clearly articulate why you want to train in the US is key because this is what is going to be the driving force of your ambition and all the sacrifices you will inevitably have to make.

For IMGs already in the US in some other capacity, being able to concisely answer this same question will also help put you in the proper mind set. I say this because the natural feeling is, 'I am a trained Medical Doctor from my home country, what else can I do aside from practice medicine?'

As IMGs, the natural expectation we harbor in our minds is to continue in a career we have dedicated so much time and resources to. To think this way is completely appropriate. However, in my opinion, this natural expectation has to give way to a mindset of aggressive ambition. As doctors, we have all harbored this aggressive mindset at some point in time. I recall how aggressive I was about getting into not just any medical school, but Nigeria's first and best - The College of Medicine University of Ibadan, Nigeria. While in medical school, I recall the ambitious aggressiveness in me each time I prepared for a major school exam. These are fond memories of early adult hood. Unfortunately, the average IMG seeks to transition into US residency at a time in our lives when we have lost some, if not all of our aggressiveness. We often begin the path to US residency in our early to late 30s, and sometimes in our 40s. At this age, we have become more mature and less excitable. We have traded the youthful impatience that stems from exuberance, for the equally damaging adult impatience that stems from knowing our time is running out. We have sometimes acquired the responsibility of having a family. It is against this back drop that we embark on the journey to US residency. Unfortunately, the rules of engagement have not changed. Things of value still have to be pursued with hard work. Getting into a US Medical School is not a walk in the park, neither is getting into a residency position. Some of us are quick to realize this and come to terms with it. We dig into our innermost reserves and re-ignite the enthusiasm needed to compete. Some of us either never come to terms with the reality we face as IMGs or do so when it is too late. A laissez-faire attitude will not suffice.

———

So, why did I want to pursue residency in the United States? I was a practicing medical doctor in Nigeria. By God's grace, I had managed to secure a surgery residency position in Lagos, Nigeria. This was no small fete (show me one country worth its salt where residency is not competitive, especially surgical specialties!). Within the first few months of my residency, I was completely dissatisfied with life in general. There was a huge divide between every day practice and what the textbooks prescribed. Aside from the usual issues of lack of appropriate technology and trained expertise that bedevils the so-called third world countries and their institutions, there were painful system problems that I just could not contend with. Granted, we saved lives and made the local community better by employing the skills and technology we had at our disposal, but the world had moved on and it was like we were not even aware. I woke up one day and knew I could not go on an extra day practicing medicine as I did back then. My ambition exceeded the opportunities available to me. My despondency paradoxically fired me up. I decided I would rather take my chances than continue in my present state. This all transpired in 2010. I started General Surgery residency in the US in 2013. Not every day of that three-year interlude were happy days. But I had burnt the bridge and there was no looking back because I knew why I left Nigeria and what I was looking for in the U.S. Knowing what I wanted kept me going. My goal was in sight and I was going to keep trudging along. You need to know why you want to be a U.S trained doctor. The relaxed response of 'there is nothing else I can do aside from practice medicine' will not suffice. There are so many non-practicing doctors in various careers in the US.

To be clear, when I talk about taking my chances, it was not an ignorant gamble. I had done some online research and I was ready to trade the known security of a surgery residency in Nigeria, for the prospects of an unknown future.

3 **CLARITY OF PURPOSE**

There is no ambition without a clarity of purpose.
You have to be clear as to what you want, only then
can you channel your energy and resources
appropriately.

It is neither unusual nor is it a bad thing to have
some indecision. But this indecision should be
short-lived. The average third year medical student
in the United States has no idea as to what sub
specialty of medicine they want to pursue. For some
students, their chosen specialty literally changes as
they move from one clinical rotation to another: this
month it is family medicine, next month it is

Ophthalmology. However, for most students, their goals begin to crystallize as they approach the end of their third year of medical school. The students who have their minds made up earlier than later, are the ones who do best at establishing the right networks among members of faculty and arranging fourth year 'sub-intern' rotations at the most opportune time that gives them good exposure to faculty. By extension, these interactions often yield good letters of recommendation towards the residency application season.

I still have my personal journal from 2009 where I stated what I wanted in life professionally. Nine years after I made that journal entry, I reflect on what I wrote, and it helps me in my self-evaluations. You have to be clear in your purpose. My journal reminded me that almost a decade ago, I actually considered being an Orthopedic Surgeon (ironically, while I was in medical school, Orthopedic surgery was one of my top three DO NOT DO specialties. The other two being Neurosurgery and ENT). This underscores the fact that even if your purpose has not taken perfect shape, it cannot be totally amorphous. Overtime, my purpose crystallized, my enthusiasm bubbled and my ambition was shaped like a flint.

————

It is not atypical for an IMG who desires to be a Dermatologist for example, to have concerns regarding their chance of U.S residency given the extremely competitive nature of Dermatology. For some IMGs, their primary interest is a surgical specialty. The IMG looks at the playing field and realizes the competition is daunting. The question then becomes, do I pursue a surgery residency against all obvious odds, or do I settle for another specialty where the odds are seemingly better? I believe having these kind of questions at the back of your mind do not reflect self-doubt, rather it demonstrates that you have at least an idea of what you are up against and that you are in tune with reality. You do not want to dive head-on into the waters of U.S residency without the slightest inkling of what the stakes are. Many IMGs have done so and ended up being irretrievably lost at sea.

Deciding early on what specialty you want to pursue helps you channel your time and resources appropriately viz. seek out mentors in the chosen field and people who will be willing to write letters of recommendation for you, engage in shadowing, and establish good networks among members of faculty in the field.

I believe being able to decide on how to proceed rests on your answer to the question: Am I competitive enough for my desired specialty?

How competitive you are is not necessarily about how good your application packet is, but how good the competition is. What are my USMLE scores and how do they compare to the average scores of other applicants in my chosen specialty? What kind of networks have I been able to establish within the field if any? Do I have or will I be able to obtain strong letters of recommendation from members of faculty in my chosen field of interest?

-Will I be happy doing anything else?

The world is full of people unfulfilled in their chosen careers. Do not add to the number. If you know a certain specialty will not make you a happy doctor, do not go into that specialty.

4 THE NUMBER ONE FLAW

My people perish for lack of knowledge. Hosea 4:6

I have spoken with several intelligent IMGs and I
have been taken aback on multiple occasions by
how very little they know about the very system of
medical practice they are trying to get into.
Knowledge is power. Technological knowledge
helped land a man on the moon. Knowledge
(intelligence) has helped capture child abductors
and terrorists. Knowledge has informed sound
investments on the stock exchange. Knowledge
from history, physical exam and radiographic
imaging helps make sound intra-operative

decisions. I once spoke with an IMG who was poised to sit for the United States Medical Licensing Examination (USMLE) Step 1 in a few days, and she did not know what the passing score was! I was shocked to say the least. A thousand questions raced through my mind in speeds my tongue could not keep up with: What are your goals in this exam? Is there a particular score you have tagged as your personal minimum? Do you know the average passing scores of all candidates? What is the average USMLE step 1 score for candidates applying to the same specialty as you plan to? Are you aware that once you attain the 'passing score' for this exam, regardless of how un-competitive your score is, you are not allowed to retake it except to comply with certain time limits (see usmle.org for more information regarding attempts, time limits and retakes).

I believe the number one flaw that undermines the IMG's ambition is knowledge based. And I do not mean a deficiency in medical knowledge, far from it! On the contrary, most IMGs are very intelligent doctors, sometimes the best from our respective countries. I believe the number one flaw is a failure to understand the extent of the challenge that IMGs face:

- Underestimating the competition
- A lack of understanding of the design (not content) of the USMLE exams
- A lack of understanding of the application process and the Match: The Match is an algorithm by the National Resident Matching Program that attempts to 'match'

an applicant with his/her most preferred residency program. Visit www.nrmp.org to read about the Match and what it means.

I am certain you can appreciate that none of these factors I enumerated has to do with the medical knowledge of the applicant. As I counsel IMGs who pick my brain in pursuit of their goals, I always tell them this: After passing, you will come to discover that passing the USMLE exams was the easiest step in the application process. IMGs who are yet to attempt the exams or have attempted and failed find it difficult coming to terms with this statement of mine. However, among those who have passed and moved on in the process towards residency, none has disagreed with this statement of mine as they jump the hurdles in the application process.

There are two types of passes. The first is when you 'pass', meaning you attained or surpassed the stipulated score that exempts you from having to re-take the exam. When it comes to getting a residency spot, absolutely no one cares if you attained this first pass or not. This is because, achieving this first 'pass' is one definite thing every single candidate has in common. Passing the USMLE is a prerequisite. There will be no conversation of a career in medicine or seeking a residency spot if you do not attain this first pass. Next, there is the other 'pass', meaning you have excelled in the exam above and beyond the baseline score that defines the first 'pass'.

Do not be fooled, competition does not begin at the first pass. The first pass exists because for any assessment test to serve its purpose, it ought to have a 'minimum' that defines pass or fail. The real competition begins after you have met the standard that defines a pass. Please do not go into the exam hall with the aim of 'I just want to pass'. IMGs who do this have missed the goal from the get-go. Given that once you pass a USMLE exam, you are not allowed to retake it except to comply with certain time limits (see usmle.org for more information regarding attempts, time limits and retakes), IMGs who attain only the first 'pass' without achieving a competitive score have essentially become committed stem cells. Like a rat in maze, they get stuck in the residency application maze. If the average IMG requires one miracle to get into residency, such candidates require a couple. I have had multiple IMGs express their frustration to me regarding the entire residency application process. I hear things like 'I have passed all the exams, including Step 3, I am ECFMG certified, yet I have not matched'. I start by asking about their exam scores to have a better understanding of what they mean by 'I have passed'. I am yet to be surprised.

———

I began researching the USMLE and Match in the second quarter of 2008. This was more than two years before my exodus from Nigeria and more than three years before I sat for USMLE step 1. I began my research by simply looking up what was required of an IMG who desired residency training in the United States. My search immediately made me acquainted with all the acronyms that foreign medical graduates eventually become familiar with (ECFMG, OASIS, IWA, ERAS, NRMP). I discovered that even IMGs can be further stratified into US IMG (meaning IMGs with a US passport or green card) and non-US IMG (IMG foreign both in training and nationality). I read about ECFMG and what the organization did. I realized ECFMG would serve as my 'Dean's office' and this administrative body was going to be my go-to for all matters regarding my desired training in the US. I read about the requirement of being ECFMG certified which meant passing USMLE step 1 as well as USMLE step 2CK and 2CS. I learnt USMLE Step 1 and Step 2CK could be written outside of the US, but I had to be physically present in the United States to sit for the USMLE Step 2CS examination. To my dismay, I discovered I could not sit for USMLE Step 1 and 2CK in Nigeria and would have to consider visiting Ghana (Nigeria's neighbor to the

West), to sit for the exams. I downloaded the NRMP Match statistics reports from the NRMP web site and went through it, focusing on General surgery but also perusing other specialties. I recall very vividly the night I went through the NRMP Match statistics. I saw the staggering numbers in the General surgery application pool and the very small fraction of IMGs who matched. The statistics split the IMG pool into US IMG and non-US IMG making the already small fraction infinitesimally smaller. Looking at those numbers and comparing the match statistics of all groups: US Seniors (US medical students in their fourth year of medical school), US graduates (previous US graduates not currently in their fourth year of medical school), Osteopathic students (Students in Osteopathic Medical schools), Students from Canadian Medical

33

Schools, US IMG , non-US IMG . It was easy to appreciate how the numbers thinned out. I realized I was at the bottom of the food chain. Nonetheless, I recall very clearly how excited I was that it was indeed do-able! The numbers were there to show that there have been IMGs who have matched into General Surgery in the US. Ambition made me believe. I highly recommend you go through the NRMP match outcomes data and see what the match trends have been over the years for your specialty of interest.

Next, I researched the residency application process. The information I gained from this homework defined the next moves I made in subsequent years. I recall reading about how the ECFMG would serve as the 'dean's office' for IMGs. I read about the requirement for letters of recommendation from members of faculty, preferably faculty in your specialty of interest. Without being told, I figured letters of recommendation from members of faculty in the US would likely be more credible. I read about the Matching process and how the algorithm works.

My research led me to two conclusions. First the competition is fierce. And this is not just because the number of applicants to a residency program is several multiples of the number of residency positions the program has (See chapter The Competition). Second, I had to be in the US when I applied for residency. Of course, I could have decided to write USMLE Steps 1 and 2CK in Ghana, then visit the US to sit for Step 2CS. But my decision stemmed from my realization of how steep the competition was AFTER passing the exam. I knew I had to up the ante in some form and I was

not going to be able to do that from 5000 miles

away.

5 **THE COMPETITION**

Know your enemy and know yourself; in a hundred

battles, you will never be defeated - Sun Tzu

While in Medical School at the University of

Ibadan, Nigeria, I applied for a National

Scholarship. Alongside thousands of other brilliant

young men and women, I was invited for a written

interview. I had done my research by asking a

colleague who had taken a similar scholarship

interview. I began preparing for the interview by

solving problems on advanced mathematics. I told

myself then: Every question you answer correctly

will be answered by thousands of examinees, and

every question you answer incorrectly will be answered correctly by thousands of examinees - giving them an edge over you. This mantra helped my keep the scope of the competition in perspective. I made the short list and got the scholarship.

Having an understanding of the competition you are up against is crucial. While researching the USMLE, the residency application process and the Match, I discovered that in the US, there were combined MD/PhD programs. This was news to me. I also learnt that some medical students took time off to obtain a master's degree in some allied health disciplines. I came to realize that a significant number had, to some degree, been involved in at least one research project with one or more publications to their credit. Aside from these extra academic pursuits, majority of students have had something extra-curricular to adorn their resume: sports with or without athletic scholarships, volunteering etc. This made me realize how attractive such candidates will be. These were the candidates I was meant to be competing with! I had no real research experience. As a House Officer at the University College Hospital (UCH) Ibadan, I had helped collect samples for a research project. But that was it: no abstract, no poster, no paper, no proof! I had been very active in my medical school press club and had risen through the ranks from Secretary to Editor-in-chief. I was a member of the college of medicine debate team and as chief speaker, we won the very first inter collegiate debate competition. I was also active on the sports track and had a couple of medals to show for it. My point being, I had a handful of extracurricular achievements. But was that enough to compete for a general surgery position? Will these touted accolades of mine make me a shining star that will stand out in an application pool of thousands of applicants, most of whom attended medical school in the US, and most of whom had impressive resumes? The year I applied for residency there were over two thousand applicants for categorical general surgery for a little over one thousand positions. What will make a program director in the United States with only a handful of residency spots to fill, give consideration to my application in a pool of a thousand applications, the majority being from students from more recognizable schools and easily verifiable credentials? I know people are naturally more comfortable with what is familiar to

them. I was not kidding myself. I knew the
University of Utah, for example, was more
recognizable than the University of Ibadan. If I
scored 270 on USMLE Step1, I knew there was
someone who will score 271 (there is always
someone better than you). I also knew there was
someone who will score 255 (lower than my
hypothetic 270) but who will still be a more
attractive candidate for reasons of strong letters of
recommendation, phone calls from members of
academia, a handful of abstracts, a manuscript or
two, and extracurricular activities. What if the
program director (PD) wanted to verify my
credentials? Was there a phone number that he
could call at my alma mata? When the PD calls at
1pm central time in the US, which would be 7 or
8pm in Nigeria, of course no one will pick up the

phone, and there most certainly was no answering phone service. What if the PD decided to send an email to my school? Would the email ever be received? Would anyone read that email? Will a reply ever be sent? If I obtained letters of recommendation from faculty in my medical school, could the PD reach them by phone to discuss how good or bad a candidate I am? (Trust me, these phone calls take place ALL the time and at ALL levels - Residency, Fellowship, Job applications. Beyond the paper application, PDs make calls to do some background check on the candidates they are most interested in or have concerns about). Given that I was an international candidate, was the program ready to take on a candidate who required a visa and were they ready to deal with the extra paper work? Even though it is an efficient system that ECFMG has in place to handle the visa requirements, many people in authority either are sincerely not aware of the near simplicity of the process or just do not want to deal the potential complex problems that may arise. I was ruminating on all these questions several years before the political discourse on travel and immigration became such a heated debate. I knew that an IMG with a green card and a score of 235 on USMLE Step 1 would likely be a more attractive candidate than myself even if I score 5 points higher. This brings me to a sub group of my competitors: IMGs resident in the US.

———

I was, 5000 miles away in Ibadan Nigeria, surveying my prospects of residency in the US. But then I came to realize there was a population of IMGs already in the US who were engaged in a multitude of ways: Post doctorate programs, pursuing a Master's degree or PHD, working in research labs and getting their names on manuscripts, working as research coordinators and networking with the people of appropriate influence, shadowing clinicians and showcasing their brilliance, or simply staying at home. These candidates were garnishing their resumes and increasing their level of familiarity. I knew what I was bringing to the table, but I also caught a glimpse of what my competition was up to, and it scared me. It dawned on me at that time, there was no question of writing USMLE Exams remotely and applying remotely. I had to have boots on the ground! Don't get me wrong. My decision to prepare and apply for the match from within the U.S was solely based on my assessment of my strengths as a candidate and the opportunities I had at my disposal. I had my eyes on a competitive specialty – General Surgery. If my cards had been stacked differently, I would have played them differently. The point I am communicating is that you need to do a thorough self-evaluation and give yourself a humble assessment of where you stand. Several IMGs have successfully matched into U.S residency programs by applying from abroad. Majority of these candidates often have something that sets them apart. It could be history of a clinical rotation in a hospital in the US, a reliable contact in a position of authority that is ready to go out on a limb on behalf of the candidate, or anything else of significant distinction. In my assessment of the playing field, I figured by attempting to apply for the match from outside the US, I would simply be making an already difficult process increasingly more difficult. My decision to prepare and apply for the match from within the U.S was based on my assessment and the opportunities I had at my disposal. I encourage you to carry out a realistic self-assessment of where you stand.

6 BRING SOMETHING EXTRA

Getting into residency is very competitive, no doubt. But it is also a well-known fact that certain specialties are more competitive than others. Generally speaking, surgical specialties are more competitive than the non-surgical specialties. A notable exception is Dermatology, which is probably more competitive than some surgical specialties. Within the field of surgery, Orthopedic surgery is known for being very competitive. I am sure you comprehend the point I am making. If you want to swim with the sharks, you had better bring your game on. Your specialty of interest will determine just how much extra you have to bring to the table. The truth is, with good USMLE scores, little or no research experience and some decent letters of recommendation, an IMG stands a good chance of getting into a non-surgical specialty in at least a good community program. Visit NRMP.org and see the proportion of IMGs that match into Internal medicine, Pediatrics and Psychiatry. For IMGs like me with more grandiose ambitions, there has to be something that gives an edge beyond good USMLE scores.

After I made the decision of writing the USMLE and turning in my application from within the US, I had to decide on what my approach will be. My desire was to get involved in some form of academic research, which is something I have always been interested in. But how do I key into some academic research? What was going to be my point of entry into the system? I could not just show up at the American Consulate requesting a visa because I had been bitten by the research bug. My quest for answers on-line led me to the popular Masters in Public Health (MPH) degree. I got in touch with an IMG in the US who was not in residency but was engaged in some activity which I cannot recall. I sent him an email asking about the bearing a master's degree has on residency application. His response was that a Masters had next to no bearing, which is largely true (I will explain further on). Nonetheless, I explored the option of a master's degree vs a PhD for three reasons. First, either of these paths would satisfy my long running desire to be involved in academic research. I hoped that the research would yield some publications and help me network with people of influence. Second, the added qualification will give me some leverage, no matter how small. Third, pursuing a degree will give me the much-needed time to prepare for and write the USMLE exams, and apply for the match. I opted for the master's degree because I just did not want to invest so much time in a PhD. I mentioned earlier that in my opinion, time is one of the biggest sacrifices one has to make in pursuit of US residency. I was more than ready to invest as much time as I needed, but I was also ready to invest no more than I required. Time was my currency, I was determined to spend it wisely. I shifted gear into searching out potential schools in the US where I could obtain a master's degree. It was at this time my ambitious goals experienced their first major setback (I discussed this in the chapter 'The battle is in the mind'). I overcame that hit and plodded on.

———————

My Alma Mata, The University of Ibadan (UI)
remains Nigeria's premier and best citadel of
learning. UI has churned out some of Nigeria's
brightest minds, including my mum, who have
made significant contributions both locally and
internationally in their field. Sadly, like Bees
irresistibly drawn to honey, UI's best and brightest
are continually attracted to places with better
opportunity. I often say the reason I left Nigeria is
because my ambition exceeded the opportunities I
had. At the time I was searching for potential
schools, there were UI trained Medical Doctors
sprinkled all over graduate schools in the US:
Minnesota, New York, Atlanta, Texas, Boston. At a

point in time there were about a dozen of my senior colleagues enrolled in Harvard. I looked in the direction of these schools with a 'UI presence' and knocked each one off the list one at a time. Cost of tuition was a major factor; another was the duration of the degree. At that time, the MPH degree at Harvard was a one-year program. This was immediately undesirable for me. Given the information I had gleaned from all my homework, I knew a one-year program will not provide adequate time for me to get my ducks lined in a row. I wanted a two-year program. I have counselled candidates who are seeking to obtain a degree while working on the USMLE and my advice is the same: ensure you have enough time. Once again, I believe it comes down to the level of knowledge and preparation, and knowing yourself. I figured if I arrived in the US in time to start a one-year MPH in the fall (August), would I be ready by the next fall (Sept) to turn in a decent application for the Match? I did not think I was going to be able to travel from one continent to another, and within one year, acclimatize to a different culture and climate, get settled into a master's program, prepare for and perform very well in USMLE Step 1, 2CK and 2CS, establish connections that will yield strong letters of recommendation from members of faculty in the US, and possibly get some academic research publications. I did not think it was impossible, I simply felt it was not feasible for me. I encourage you to know yourself, your God given talents and the opportunities at your disposal.

———

After doing all my homework on potential affordable schools, I decided I wanted to attend a College of Public Health that was actively involved with physicians or had physicians as members of faculty. This was a big gamble since I could only glean so much from the information provided on-line. I also wanted a College that would provide some form of financial scholarship. All the schools that offered financial scholarship required the Graduate Record Examination (GRE). Unfortunately, as I mentioned earlier, I had experienced a major setback that made me feel I needed to suspend my ambition to travel to the US for a while. As at the time I recovered from this momentary setback, I felt I did not have sufficient time to prepare for the GRE and obtain a very competitive score. Once again, I was frank with myself. With time, we all know what we are capable of, at least I do, and I do not think more highly of myself than I ought. This time constraint sent me back to the drawing board. I knocked off all schools that required a GRE. I eventually settled on the University of Oklahoma and it was perfect! I could afford the tuition, the College of Public Health was actively engaged in clinical research with physicians, it was a quiet place where I could keep my head down and focus, and importantly, I had family in Oklahoma! (I will talk more about the impact having family close by had in my progress in the chapter 'We all need help on our way up').

With my sights set on the University of Oklahoma (OU), I began to zero in on the extra I was bringing to the table. I sent in my application to the College of Public Health and by God's grace I was accepted.

Before I ever set my foot on the steps of the College of Public Health, I had my goals outlined: I was going to do well, get involved in a research and get recognized. This gives me another opportunity to reiterate the importance of having a clarity of purpose. I knew what I wanted. I did not have all the answers to how, but I knew the answers to why. Also, I cannot over emphasize the importance of investing the time to do some homework, plan and prepare. Let me share another vivid memory. I recall sitting in my house in Lagos, Nigeria and going through a publication of the OU College of Public Health. In that issue, they celebrated two or three students that graduated with a GPA of 4.0. They had a grade of A in every single class! To me this was unheard off. The Nigerian educational curriculum is different from that of the US in several respects. One of the differences is that perfection is unattainable in the Nigerian system. While I was at the University of Ibadan, Nigeria, a grade of 'A' starts at 70 and it is almost nearly impossible to achieve an 'A' in a single class. Making an 'A' in every class was definitely impossible. Sitting there in Lagos, I knew I wanted to graduate with a GPA of 4.0 from the OU College of Public Health.

———

I resumed in OU in the spring of 2011 and I hit the ground running. Not long after the commencement of the semester, I spoke with a member of faculty about my desire to be a graduate research assistant (GRA). She did not have any offers. She also informed me it was difficult to offer such positions to a new student given that I had no antecedent aside from my application credentials. She did point me in the direction of other members of faculty. I fired off a few emails. None yielded any success. I pursued my studies with vigor. At the end of the semester, I was offered a position as a graduate teaching assistant. I also finished off my first semester with a GPA of 4.0. At the end of my second semester, I was offered the position of a graduate research assistant (GRA). I took up this offer. I maintained both my position as a GRA and my GPA of 4.0 over the next 3 semesters till I graduated. I was accumulating my extras.

I believe my getting the job as GRA was predicated on several factors, two of which were my academic performance and my work ethic as a teaching assistant. (See the chapter 'We all need help on our way up' for my thoughts on other factors). Getting the job as GRA opened the doors to the 'extras' I was seeking. I got involved in several research projects and got my name on a manuscript and a few abstracts. I got to meet several people of influence who played very significant roles in the actualization of my dream. My extras were not many, but they were not zero either. I knew I had competitors who had decorated their resumes in a more colorful fashion and had established much more extensive networks than I had. I could not focus on that though. I had drawn my game plan, I was following through, and lines were falling in pleasant places. I was simply grateful. It is essential that you pick your battles and fight them. Identify what extras you will be bringing to the table, map out a plan to achieve them, then give it all your all.

Be ambitious but set realistic goals.

Today, I often get asked the same question I asked that young man years ago: how much will a master's degree help me get into a residency? And my response is this: it depends on what you get out of the master's degree. If the master's degree gives you research experience, publications and helps you network, then go for it because that would make a significant difference. If your goal is to simply acquire the degree and stamp it on your application, it may not necessarily help that much. It all depends on how competitive your specialty of interest is. Almost every IMG has a master's degree, some have PhDs! If you set your eyes on one of the big-name schools, be careful not to get lost in the crowd. Your brilliant plan to adorn your resume with a degree from an ivy league school has been conceived and hatched by many an IMG. Some people will go to these prestigious named but saturated schools, achieve good success and launch out from there, but most will not. It has nothing to do with how gifted you are, it is simply the law of demand and supply. Take the time to seek out areas of opportunity.

Beyond my personal experience, there are candidates who have improved their attractiveness in ways other than a postgraduate degree. Some have worked in research labs while others have simply had the opportunity to shadow doctors in the US, and this has opened up doors for them. Some candidates have tapped into relationships and networks that they were fortunate enough to have. All that matters is that you seek out opportunities to become more competitive for your chosen specialty of interest and maximize the opportunities presented to you knowing that every second counts. The clock is ticking!

7 **PREPARING FOR THE USMLES**

As I worked hard to improve my resume, I was simultaneously preparing for the USMLE. I started preparing for USMLE Step 1 in the spring of 2011. I was enrolled in 16 credit hours in the MPH program. Despite being my first exposure to the American educational system, I was determined to have a GPA of 4.0 and do well in the USMLE. I knew that having a good score did not guarantee I will match, but I was also certain that having a poor score will most definitely shut the doors of opportunity and lock me in the rat race. How do I expect to be given a chance to practice medicine in the US if I do not perform well in the very first basic requirement? As an IMG, the odds were already stacked against me. Why would I seal my fate with a poor performance and expect to be preferred above others? If I was a program director of a residency program in Nigeria, will I favor an international medical graduate from a school I never heard of, with less than impressive licensing exam scores, over a Doctor (regardless of nationality) who trained in a recognizable Nigerian school and has competitive scores? The exams serve several purposes some of which are to create uniformity and a level playing field, and to weed out candidates. These standardized tests seek to form a basis of comparison for medical students from diverse schools across the US who have been educated using different curricula. Regardless of the criticism of standardized tests, we are yet to find a better surrogate. By taking these tests, IMGs are being placed on the same pedestal as the US medical students. If I failed to pass the examination, that begs the question: Are there gaps in my knowledge base that will make me inadequate to pursue further training and practice medicine in the US? After all, over 90% of US-graduates pass USMLE step 1 at their first attempt while a little over 70% of IMGs pass USMLE step 1 at their first attempt. These numbers have largely remained unchanged for several years. Visit the USMLE website and review the performance data. I do not know all the reasons why a large number of IMGs perform poorly on the USMLE but from my discussions with individuals who have failed or done poorly, the common reasons I could deduce were: a lack of understanding of the structure (not content) of the USMLE exams and a lack of proper preparation. I was determined to do well on the USMLE. But what defines well?

Do your homework

As always, I began with some homework. I built upon my previous research and searched for more information on line. I cannot over emphasize the importance of knowledge. I reviewed the USMLE bulletin of information. I scoured the internet for the average scores and what score ranges defined good scores. The popular USMLE First AID book for Step 1 has a chart showing competitive scores according to specialty. These simple details are vital to getting in the proper mind set. It also helps you set your goals. A while ago, an acquaintance sent me an email asking if I would be kind enough to speak with an IMG who was harboring thoughts of residency and medical practice in the US. I spoke with the gentleman and from our conversation, it was evident he did not know much about the process. This is okay! Everyone starts from somewhere. After a lengthy conversation, I suggested reading the USMLE bulletin of information will be a good place to begin to comprehend what is expected of him, so I sent him the link. Three months after that encounter, he was yet to read the bulletin. You have to invest the time in preparation and knowledge gathering. Proper preparation prevents poor performance! This was harped in my ears while growing up.

The structure of the USMLE

I will never forget the first USMLE styled question I ever read. I was in Lagos in 2010 ruminating on plans for the future. I had earlier purchased an uncommon edition of one of the numerous USMLE preparatory books available on the market. This was an ignorant purchase. I say this to underscore the importance of doing your homework. I simply walked into a book store and purchased the said book. The book is so uncommon, I have never heard its name mentioned by anyone in reality or on-line. And I never really used the book. It paled in comparison to the popular Kaplan and First Aid series. I was passing time one day, so I flipped the book open. I will never forget that moment. The question was on the left bottom corner of a random

page I opened. The vignette was of an individual

who had a constellation of symptoms. As I read

through, I got increasingly excited because 'I could

see' where the question was going. I had put all the

symptoms together and identified the syndrome as

Multiple Endocrine Neoplasia I (MEN I). I don't

know if you have ever experienced the feeling I

had. A feeling of excitement and anticipation when

you know you are on the right track. As I read on, I

was eager to get to the bottom of the vignette where

I was certain the question would end with "what is

the diagnosis?". I had my answer ready on my lips.

Even though it was just one question, knowing that

I had opened up to a random question, without any

dedicated study time, and I had cracked the code so

easily, made me feel the USMLE is not that hard

after all. If I could answer this question so easily, it would only get better when I began targeted studying towards the USMLE. I continued reading the vignette and my heart sunk when I read the last phrase: "what is the mode of inheritance?". I had no idea! I had read of the MEN syndrome in my texts but I had never really paid attention to its mode of inheritance. The focus had always been knowing the symptoms that constituted the syndrome. What really shocked me was the structure of the question. Wow! In one paragraph, this question had tested my knowledge at two levels. The first test was to see if I could identify the pattern in the patient's symptoms and make a diagnosis. If I did not make a diagnosis, I did not advance to the next level and my final answer would be a random guess. I had made a diagnosis, but then I got stopped in my tracks at level two: the mode of inheritance. I analyzed my performance and realized that by failing to know the pattern of inheritance at level two, I was as good as someone else who never made a diagnosis at level one. My half knowledge was of no use to me. This was a seminal moment for me. At that moment, I realized this exam was a living, intelligent being. This pattern of examination was unfamiliar to me, and I am yet to meet an IMG who has expressed previous familiarity with this style of testing. I believe testing in this unfamiliar fashion is a major factor in the performance of IMGs in the USMLE, especially Step 1. In my opinion, to do well on Step 1, two things are required of you. First you have to understand the multilayered structure of the questions as I just explained. Some questions are relatively straight forward and do not follow this pattern of complexity. On the other hand, there are some questions that are intricately designed to test the examinee's knowledge base on up to 3 levels. You have to carefully read the vignette and peel away at the core of the question layer by layer. If you don't peel away the first layer, you don't make a dent in the question. If you peel away layer one but fail to peel back layer two, then you get buried. My advice is this - make a diagnosis! If you can make a diagnosis at some point, chances are you will be able to answer the question correctly. When the vignette presents a young female with certain symptoms, and a gram stain of certain characteristics - make a diagnosis! Without making a diagnosis of what organism is in question, you will be clueless as to what antibiotic choice to make at the end of the question stem. When the vignette

presents a young man with a prior history

of dysphagia and regurgitation and an out pouching

in the cervical esophagus on barium swallow,

who now has neck swelling and pain after receiving

surgical treatment for his condition - make a

diagnosis! Only then will you be able to answer

correctly what complication of treatment the patient

has suffered. Understanding the structure of the

USMLE is essential. What I have just described is

common to all USMLE questions, especially Step

1. The second thing is, you have to beef up your

knowledge base extensively. This comes only by

investing the time to study. There is no way round

this. I strongly advice answering a ton of practice

questions prior to the exam, but this is by no means

a substitute for studying. I have met candidates who

spend all the time answering questions with little time apportioned for studying. I don't recommend this. The questions help to challenge your understanding of your knowledge base. Questions are not the primary mode of increasing your knowledge base, only studying does that.

USMLE Step 2CS and the 'clinical encounter' aspects of Step 3 are different in the sense that they are not the typical multiple choice questions (see USMLE.org for official content description of these exams). Even the examining body knows that understanding the structure of the exams is essential, that is why they have provided a clear description of these exams on their website as well as sample questions and scenarios. There is a reason these materials have been provided!

The sequence of the exams

Though you may sit for the exams in any sequence, there is a reason Step 1 comes before Step 2. I know several IMG's who have sat for Step 2CS and/or 2CK before step 1. If this works for you, good. However, my take is this; there is a reason those exams are structured the way they are (see USMLE.org). Even after you have passed Step 2 and your confidence level is improved (an argument people often make for taking Step 2CS first), Step 1 will still be waiting. There is a reason Step 1 is a rate-limiting step. I encourage you to take the exams in the sequence they were intended to be taken.

Getting yourself ready to write the exam

- You have to study hard. There is no short cut around it. You need to invest those hours staring at the pages of books. I have emphasized the importance of studying as well as practicing questions. To avoid endorsing any particular brand of preparatory materials, I advise speaking with people who you know have taken the exam. Seek their opinion and recommendations. There are some very popular and reputable materials out there, you need not look too far before you encounter them.

- Talk with other candidates about their exam preparation experience. I did not have this opportunity when preparing for my exams and I wish I had. I did all my studying alone. It was not until my preparation for Step 2CS, did I find someone I could role play with in practice for the test.

- Know about the exam you are preparing for. Know the length of the exam and how much break time you will have. Plan your exam day. When I was preparing for Step 1, I knew exactly between which exam blocks I planned to take my breaks and for how long. Be prepared. I also knew (by extensive online foraging) that results of Step 1 where often released on the third Wednesday after your exam day. To shorten my period of anxious waiting, I chose to write my exam on a Monday morning. The Wednesday after my exam counted as the first Wednesday, thereafter all I needed to do was find a way to survive two weeks of waiting. Be smart, be informed, be knowledgeable.

- Answer a ton of practice questions from a good question bank. There is unarguably one question bank that is largely considered the best question bank for the USMLE. My guiding principle was to review a total number of practice questions 10 times the number of questions on the real exam. So for an exam of say 200 questions, my goal was 2000 practice questions. If you study hard and use the practice questions the way they are meant, you improve your chance of having a good score. A colleague of mine from medical school in Nigeria wrote Step 1 and failed. While talking with him, he made this comment: 'I answered all the questions in the question bank. Of all those questions, not a single one of them showed up on the exam'. The instant he made that statement, in my mind I knew he had already failed the exam long before he stepped into the exam hall. We both attended the same medical school. The way we were examined back then, the questions were often recycled verbatim. Sometimes, 100% of a test could be the exact same questions that were on a previous test from a few years back. As such, if you were lucky to acquire a bunch of previous exam questions, chances are, a significant number of those old questions (if not all) would be on the real test thus putting you in a really good position. Students sought out those old questions not so they could learn from them, but so they could recognize the answers if and when these old questions showed up on a subsequent test. This friend of mine was preparing for the USMLE with the same mindset. He was answering questions in the q-bank with the mindset that some of those questions would show up on the real exam. No better recipe for failure! The question bank is not a bunch of questions that you memorize in case they show up on your exam. Those questions are designed to expose you to the format of the exam, show you critical concepts, help challenge your knowledge base, and align your thought process towards making a diagnosis and solving the problem. I can confidently wager that concepts tested in the question bank my friend used were tested in the real exam. He only did not realize it.

- Take a National Board of Medical Examiners (NBME) practice test. These tests are a veritable reflection of where you stand in the real test. If you do not pass the NBME preparatory test, I encourage you to think real hard before taking the exam. I know people who failed the NBME practice exam yet went ahead to take the real test. The outcome was predictable. Let us think this through logically. You failed a practice test that is designed to mirror the real test, yet you expect to pass the real test? If you pass the real test after failing the practice test, (and by pass I am not referring to passing by the scruff of the neck) does that not question the legitimacy of the practice test? To date, I am not aware that the legitimacy of the NBME clinical assessment tests are in question. I believe the NBME practice tests serve two primary purposes: to help you gauge where you stand performance wise in the real exam, and to expose you to the mental reality of an 8-hour exam. Even though the duration of the NBME practice test is just 4 hours, the test shows you just how mentally tasking sitting at a computer for several hours can be, especially when at every moment of that 4-hour time span, you will be critically solving problems. I always encourage candidates to take it as a REAL exam. Dedicate 4 uninterrupted hours to taking the test. Forget about social media and checking your email. Resist the urge to pull up a textbook as reference in the middle of a practice test. Get a baby sitter for your kids while you take the test. Allow yourself strictly timed, scheduled bathroom breaks. If passing the USMLE very well means anything to you, then address it with all seriousness. I recall taking an NBME practice test ahead of USMLE Step 1. I locked myself away to take the test. By the fourth hour, I was mentally fatigued and I rushed through the final block of questions. I missed some questions that I ought not to have missed, if only I had the patience to think it through.

But mentally I was burnt out! I just wanted to get up and be done with it. I realized that day, that I had to be mentally and physically ready for the real exam. I was not going to spend all the time studying only to be short changed by physical and mental fatigue on D-day.

- You cannot stop time. Set a realistic calendar based on how much time you have on your hands and a humble assessment of your God-given abilities. Do all you can to be ready. A colleague from Medical School got in touch with me asking for counsel regarding writing the USMLE and getting a residency spot. I gave my candid opinion regarding preparing for the USMLE and the Match. She informed me of her plan to write

USMLE Step 1, Step 2 CS and CK within an impressively short time frame. I told her in my opinion it was doable though I would not advice it, and I gave my reasons based on our discussion. She felt slighted by my advice and told me I was under estimating her abilities. I apologized profusely and I reiterated that I believe anything is possible if you believe and you work hard. I was simply giving advice. Shortly thereafter, she sat for USMLE Step 1 and scored less than 200. She was devastated. This had a profoundly demoralizing effect on her. Reality set in. She slowed down and did not write Step 2 CK until almost 2 years after her attempt at Step 1. She made a decent score on Step 2 CK. Needless to say, the harm was done. She was a committed stem cell. She had 'passed' Step 1. I will talk more about the USMLE exams later on in the book but let me say this: it is possible to write the USMLE exams on whatever timetable you set for yourself, short or long. It depends on your God given talents, your background knowledge and how much time you have at your disposal for purposeful preparation. Her Step 1 score would go on to hunt her. She went through the frustrating process of applying for residency multiple times. She eventually matched after her third application. Three years of valuable time, money and emotions wasted. If only she had invested a little more time from the very beginning, she may have had a better Step 1 score and the story just might be different. I

believe a good way to start is by asking

yourself, when do I want to apply for

residency? I chose 2012 as my target year of

application. I began my master's degree in

spring 2011. Given that I was taking 16

credit hours, my goal was to take USMLE

Step 1 during the summer break, specifically

July. My secondary target was, to take the

exam most definitely before resuming for

the fall semester. I wrote the exam in August

a few weeks before the commencement of

the fall semester. My next goal was to take

Step 2CS over the Christmas break,

however, I could not get an exam date over

the Christmas holiday, so I settled for the

next holiday - spring break 2012. I needed to

take the exam during a holiday break because I would need to travel out of Oklahoma to sit for the exam and I did not want to miss any of my classes. This translated into writing mid semester exams, then travelling the following week to sit for the CS exam. Not getting a date for CS in Dec 2012 ultimately altered the personal calendar/time line I had set for myself. Despite having to sit for the CS exam in Spring 2012, I knew I had to ensure my original plan to sit for Step 2CK in June 2012 remained the same. Reason being, I wanted to take my last exam at least two months before the application season to avoid any delays in score reporting. All I can say is, it took a lot of hard work, discipline and the grace of God to write these exams while maintaining a GPA of 4.0, hold a job as a graduate research assistant, and on the weekends offer private tutor sessions in Biostatistics (see chapter 'We all need help on our way up'). I have had this same 'set a calendar' spill with several candidates. It is hard to do, I know! There is family, kids, Masters degrees, PhDs, parties, cook outs and all the other important things. There are also the great distractions of social media and reality TV. Life will get in the way, that is what life does. But you also have to make demands on life. It is not impossible to address all the important things yet make time to achieve your goals. People are doing it every day.

You only need to prioritize what is important to you. I spoke with a good friend and colleague of mine when he just arrived in the US. I discussed all my talking points. I also brought up the subject of creating a personal calendar/time line and sticking to it. Several years have passed since that conversation. He has completed his master's degree and has changed job at least once since completing his master's degree. We got talking while I was working on this book. He told me he was trying to make time to study for the USMLE but it has been so difficult making the time. In his words, "I thought I was busy when I was enrolled in the master's program". He has even less time now, and that is just life. I ran into another acquaintance while working on this book. She went on and on about how life as a graduate student makes studying for the USMLE difficult. Good things often come with some measure of difficulty, otherwise they lose their value. God has blessed us all with a measure of intelligence. He has also blessed us with 24 hours every day. It is up to us to harness our God given talents and make the best of the time we have. We do not acquire knowledge from books by diffusion, rather by sacrificing those long hours to stare at the pages of books in an effort to understand what is being communicated. This is followed by sacrificing even more time, to imprint those ever-elusive facts and details on your memory, by revising what was previously studied. If only we knew how much time sportsmen and athletes put into their craft before they show up on the world stage. I recall meeting a candidate who wanted to know what study materials I used for Step 1. After sharing details of my study materials and texts with him, his response was 'that is going to take a long time to study'. It has been six years since we had that conversation, I am not aware that he eventually wrote all his exams. From China to South Africa, everyone has the same amount of time in a day to do as they will: 24 hours, no more! You chose what you want to spend your time on.

8 THE RESIDENCY APPLICATION PROCESS

The application process is yet another area that IMGs shoot themselves in the foot. Life is competitive and sometimes all you need to get ahead of the competition is being able to put a strong foot forward first. Take the time of residency application for example. We all know the application season opens in September. On a certain day, at a certain time, all candidates can turn in their applications on line. When you turn in your application, you are simply depositing it in an electronic 'mailbox'. This mailbox remains open from Sept till about April/May (when the application cycle typically closes) for all applicants to deposit their application packets. In this time frame, residency programs can visit the mailbox and retrieve (download) all the applications specifically sent to them. Take for example a PD who visits the mail box on Sept 25 and finds say 100 applications. He may choose to visit the box once a week for the next few weeks, each time downloading more applications. This means by the end of Oct, the PD may have as many as 400 applications (This is a very conservative estimate I am throwing out there. A program may receive as many as 1000 applications or more depending on the specialty and the residency program). The PD then must sort through these 400 applications to offer interviews to candidates who will eventually match into his 10 available residency positions. Chances are, if this

PD chooses to interview 100 applicants, he will most likely find 100 desirable, stellar applicants in his pool of 400. He laboriously selects these 100 competitive applicants and sends emails inviting them to interview on any of four interview dates offered between November and January. 100 of the invited applicants accept the invite (at this stage, it is so early in the interview season, everyone always accepts the invitation). Of the 300 applicants remaining from the initial pool of 400, the PD may choose an additional 25 competitive candidates and place them on a 'wait list'. As such, by the end of October, the PD has 100 candidates scheduled to interview and 25 on the wait list. How much of a chance do you think you have when you send in your application to that same program in November? Why should a PD who has 125 competitive applications, bother to download an additional 600 applications (including yours) that have piled up in the mailbox since he last visited the box? At the time your late application was being sent in, the PD and program coordinator are busy coordinating the logistics for the upcoming interviews: the emails to candidates, parking instructions, information for hotel accommodation, best places to visit while in the city, best dining spots, directions to the hospital, and instructions for the dinner the day prior to the interview. There is so much going on! The PD can wager that, if the candidate was so good and had a great application, chances are the candidate would have turned in that application early. The fact that a program proudly announces on their website that 'application closes in Jan or Feb' should mean little to you. The fate of the residency application cycle was likely sealed

long before then. Even though all these dates and

numbers I have presented are hypothetical, you can

appreciate my point. Think of it, some programs

have their interview dates posted on their website,

yet it is not impossible to apply to that program

AFTER their last interview date. Does that suggest

a new interview date will be set up for you? It is a

centralized system of application. You can send

your applications to the central mail box for as long

as the mail box is working. It simply means your

application is 'available' to the program. This does

not translate to your application being downloaded

by your program of interest. As you prepare your

application, program directors and program

coordinators are also preparing for the application

season. When the application season opens, the

programs are ready to begin to receive and sort through applications. These programs expect the candidate would be ready to turn in a complete application and anything short of this, smacks of an unprepared candidate. Create your calendar, mark your deadlines, and work tirelessly towards meeting those deadlines. Do not be the candidate that writes a USMLE exam in August a few weeks before the commencement of the application season, then begins to get antsy about the results coming out in time (despite the fact that the governing body of the exam clearly states it may take several weeks for results to be made available). When results come out, the candidate then gets apprehensive about receiving his ECFMG certificate. Eventually he turns in a complete application in late Oct or early Nov, or he updates a previously incomplete application by adding the deficient documents.

Then he complains about not getting a single

interview. One whole year lost! Don't shoot

yourself in the foot. The future belongs to those

who prepare for it.

9 THE BATTLE IS IN THE MIND

Keep thy heart will all diligence, for out of it are the issues of life
— Psalm 4:23

As I searched for a school to pursue my master's

degree, I was completely overwhelmed at the cost

of tuition! At the exchange rate of Nigeria's Naira to

the US Dollar, I would be required to cough up

millions of Naira every semester, and this was aside

from the costs of housing, feeding, textbooks,

clothing et al. This was at a time when both my

parents were retired. Some events in life get

imprinted on your memory. One such event was the

day I sat at the computer and calculated the

financial cost of obtaining an MPH. To say the

least, my heart sunk. I began to consider giving up

on the prospect of travelling to the US, at least not in the foreseeable future. Two years later, I had saved enough money to pay my tuition, and I had some extra for living expenses. Did I spend some of my money in satisfying some of my material cravings as well as have some fun? Most definitely! But I saved the bulk of it knowing in my mind that I still wanted to pursue my dreams. Though the dream appeared unattainable initially, I kept dreaming and kept working towards the dream.

The financial burden of preparing for the USMLE is real, neither is it small. I do not have an answer to how every candidate can address the financial challenges they face. I took out a personal loan when it was time for me to apply for residency. As I work on this book, I am currently mentoring an IMG who has been experiencing some real financial challenges. I heard of another IMG who after writing all the USMLEs, did not have the financial resources to apply for a residency spot. I do not have an answer for the different financial problems that beset the IMG. My advice is for you to identify and harness the opportunities you have, and plan well. Every candidate will have opportunities that differ from the next. Making the most of the opportunities you have sometimes makes all the difference.

When you look at the statistics of IMGs who match into their desired specialty, it is easy to get disillusioned - don't! Preserve and protect your mind. If you do not believe you have a chance, why give it a try? If the battle is lost in your mind, it is hard to win in reality. One of my most despondent times was in Jan 2012. I had written USMLE Step 1 and got a decent score. But then, here I was in the year 2012, the very year I planned to apply for the match and there were still so many missing pieces. Who will write me a decent letter of recommendation? Will I perform well in my upcoming USMLE Step 2 CS and CK? Will my resume be more impressive come September? I almost gave up. There was no one close by who could understand what I was going through. I had given up an equally hard-earned surgical residency in Lagos Nigeria for the prospect of residency in the US, but it all appeared like it was a pipe dream. I ran to my source of strength – God and my faith in Jesus Christ and found encouragement. I will always look back on those first three days of 2012 with gratitude to God.

10 FAILING THEORIES

For as long as the number of residency applicants outnumber the available US residency positions, some people will not match. It is the painful truth both at the residency and fellowship level. Visit NRMP.org and review the match statistics. You will see how many US medical students who either do not match into their desired specialty, or do not match at all. I have met so many US medical students who failed to match into their desired specialty and had to scramble into an alternative discipline as a last-ditch effort. Some of these students end up filling up preliminary general surgery positions to tide the year through, then reapply the following year. People who are not informed enough or who bury their head in the sand will be proponents of all sorts of theories. I will share a few that I have heard

'Asians have a better match experience because of nepotism'. I heard this and asked myself, does it count for anything that among the IMG pool, candidates of Asian descent tend to have really impressive USMLE scores and resumes? People believe whatever they want to believe.

'Some residency programs receive money from foreign countries and in return match candidates from those countries, some of who cannot speak English'. This is one of the most absurd statements I ever heard. Interestingly it was made by an US trained medical student who had failed repeatedly to

match into surgery even after completing two years in a Pre-liminary General Surgery residency spot. Even US graduates do not match!

I consider the above two theories to be the most absurd I have heard. Even if there is some truth to either of those statements, it is not the entire story. I am yet to hear conspiracy theories from someone who successfully matched into their desired residency. Do not fall into the class of those who spin all sorts of theories.

11 WHEN EXAMS DON'T GO OUR WAY

Success is not final; failure is not fatal; it is the courage to continue that counts

-Winston Churchill

Sometimes, despite our best effort, exams don't go our way and we struggle with our emotions. I have been there. Defeat is a bitter pill to swallow. It can, but does not have to be a dream killer. There are so many success stories born out of multiple previous failures. My favorite is Thomas Edison. I read his biography just after finishing medical school in Nigeria and I still keep that book on my shelf as a reminder of what purposeful persistence can achieve. Years after I read Edison's biography, I drove through Menlo Park, New Jersey (Menlo park is where Thomas Edison had his laboratory). I was yet to get into residency at the time but being in the same geographical location where Edison had demonstrated his genius was so exciting for me.

Earlier in the book, I discussed the multiple reasons I obtained a Master's degree in Public Health. Somewhere at the back of my mind, that degree was one of my 'back up plans' in case I encountered a detour or two along the path to residency. I encourage you to have a backup plan.

I know that of my medical school graduating class that remains in Nigeria, almost 100% have continued in clinical practice either as primary health care providers or as specialists in different sub-specialties of medicine. Unfortunately, not every IMG who comes over to the US will transition into clinical practice in the US. I know several IMGs who are pursuing careers in academia, health care management and other non-clinical fields. Many have promising careers in these fields. That is the opportunity the United States affords. However, I cannot comment on their perceived happiness or sense of career fulfillment. I have come to believe that the emotion of being happy is constant. But what makes us happy changes with the seasons. At some point it was amusement parks and candy, later it was college parties and good grades, then it was our first car. Later happiness was defined by the girl/boy of our dreams and money in the bank. Sadly, happiness sometimes eludes us because we are yet to achieve that 'singular thing' that we think will truly make us happy. In reality, happiness has multiple 'S.I Units'. Some units carry more weight than others. The good news is, WE decide on what makes us happy and WE determine the value of the multiple indices of happiness. Whatever your chosen S.I Units of happiness, all that matters is your realize what is truly important to you and you live happy.

12 WE ALL NEED HELP ON OUR WAY UP

We all need help on our way up.

-Ronnie Taylor PAC

A good friend of mine needed some help in his career, so I reached out to one of our physician assistants. Ronnie is a very nice gentleman and it has been a pleasure working with him. After Ronnie offered my friend the help that was needed, I sent a text to Ronnie saying thank you. He replied saying "We all need help on our way up". This idea was not new to me in any way. As a matter of fact, I am a firm believer in the concept of 'destiny helpers' (people you meet at strategic points in your life who help propel you in no small way towards fulfillment of your goals in life). But that text from Ronnie struck a chord in me. Everyone needs help. I have received help and I still need help. I am even more eager to help others.

It is against this backdrop that I have deliberately left this chapter to the very end because I believe that, after you have done all you possibly can to make yourself competitive, you still need help. Excellent students from Ivy League schools still need help - at the least, they need people to write colorful letters of recommendation on their behalf. After all they cannot write their own letters of recommendation.

I am where I am today simply by the grace of God. My help has come from God and from all the fantastic people God has placed in my path.

To me, FMG stands not just for Foreign Medical Graduate, but also Favor, Mercy, Grace! My firm faith in Jesus Christ has seen me through the most challenging times. I have been very fortunate to meet several people in life who have rendered tremendous support towards the achievement of my goals. My mentor in the College of Public Health was extremely supportive of my career goals and she remains so to this day. There was nothing I did to ensure that I met the right people at the right time. I believe all those encounters were orchestrated by God. All I did (and still do) was to work hard to position for myself for success in readiness for opportunities that came along the way. Success is born when preparation meets opportunity. The way I see life, so much is out of my hands, so I will simply focus on doing the best I can in the little I have control over. You cannot force people to write letters of recommendation for you or make a call or two on your behalf. As an IMG, you cannot force anyone to take a chance with you. What you can do is to harness your God given talents, discipline yourself and be diligent. Thereafter, it's out of your hands. What other people call luck, I ascribe to FMG – Favor (an act of kindness beyond what is due), Mercy (compassion), Grace (the free and unmerited favor of God). I remain eternally grateful to God for everything he has done and continues to do for me.

―――――――

I chose the University of Oklahoma for my master's degree for two reasons. First, OU met all my set criteria (see chapter "Bring something extra").

Second, my brother was living in Oklahoma. This

meant so much to me. I was making a big inter-

continental relocation and having family nearby was

indispensable. My brother is not in the medical

field, so all the career plans I outlined to him were

foreign ideas. I took care of all I needed to do to

advance my career, but simply having him there

cushioned the culture shock. I remain indebted to

him. I highly recommend utilizing existing

relationships (family and friends) while establishing

new networks as you inch your way up.

As I write this book, I have been reflecting on all

the multiple tasks I was joggling while working on

the USMLE. I reflect on the strict schedules I kept

just so I could keep up my grades in the master's

program, remain diligent in my duties as a GRA, be

available to the students I tutored privately in Biostatistics and also be the best I could be in the USMLE. The days were long, the hours of study gruesome, but God remained faithful! I could not have pulled it off if not for God being there. Psalm 127:1 "Unless the Lord builds the house, the builders labor in vain".

I have received help and I am so eager to help. A few years ago, a friend put me in contact with a young medical doctor fresh out of medical school in Nigeria. She was still in Nigeria and was looking forward to transitioning to the US. I began to mentor her. She eventually relocated to the US and we kept up our communication. She wrote her USLMEs, sent me her personal statement for my opinion, and turned in her application. I was beside myself with excitement when she told me she matched. As I write this book, I have never met this young lady but I feel like she is my baby sister and I am so proud of her success. I am really hoping other candidates I am currently mentoring will have stories like hers. Like I mentioned, I have counselled IMGs from so many diverse countries and the desire to help even more is what spurred me to write this book with the hope that I will be able to reach a larger audience. I hope this book helps in some little way.

EPILOGUE

I continue to apply all the core principles I have
espoused in this book

-Knowledge

-Planning and preparation

-Help from those above and around you.

-Help others

-Faith in God

I began my General surgery residency knowing that
I wanted to be a Cardiothoracic surgeon. I worked

hard to be the best I could be. Of the things within my control, I did the best I could. The things out of my control? I cast my worries on Jesus. I began to do some background digging. I learnt I could apply for fellowship in my fourth year of residency. I learnt about the importance of the ABSITE (American Board of Surgery In-training Exam) and studied hard for it, especially in my third year of General surgery residency. I discussed my plans with members of faculty. I put my faith in God: if he could do it once, he could do it again, He never fails, He has never failed. I met people who were ready to support me in my career pursuits. By God's grace, I got inducted into two prestigious societies: The Gold Humanism Honor Society and Alpha Omega Alpha. When application season commenced, I turned in my application for

Cardiothoracic fellowship on time. From my humble abode in Oklahoma, I toured the US and interviewed alongside many talented competitors from some of the most reputable hospitals. I interviewed at some of the best hospitals in the US and by extension, the world, including Baylor Houston, Cornell, Pittsburgh, Vanderbilt, Brigham and Womens', NYU, University of Washington, Baylor Dallas. I matched at the world-famous Texas Heart Institute, Baylor College of Medicine Houston. I get to walk the same halls, where the duo of Michael DeBakey and Denton Cooley, Cardiac surgery giants of our time, made history. I am humbled when I think of my path thus far, from Lagos Nigeria to Baylor College of Medicine, Houston. Yes, I am an FMG. I am the epitome of Favour, Mercy and Grace!

Making The Match

Made in the USA
Las Vegas, NV
20 August 2021